Shiner

About the author

Maggie Nelson is a poet, critic, and award-winning author of *The Argonauts*, *Bluets*, *The Art of Cruelty*, *Jane: A Murder* and *The Red Parts*. She lives in Los Angeles, California.

Shiner

MAGGIE NELSON

ZED

This edition of *Shiner* is published by arrangement with
Hanging Loose Press, 231 Wyckoff Street Brooklyn,
New York 11217-2208, USA.

www.hangingloosepress.com

This edition published in 2018 by Zed Books Ltd,
The Foundry, 17 Oval Way, London SE11 5RR, UK.

www.zedbooks.net

Typeset in Haarlemmer MT by seagulls.net
Cover design by Alice Marwick

A catalogue record for this book is available from the
British Library

ISBN 978-1-78699-465-3 pb
ISBN 978-1-78699-466-0 pdf
ISBN 978-1-78699-467-7 epub
ISBN 978-1-78699-468-4 mobi

Printed and bound by CPI Group (UK) Ltd, Croydon CR0 4YY

MIX
Paper from
responsible sources
FSC® C020471
www.fsc.org

for my father, Bruce A. Nelson
1943–1984

Contents

Acknowledgements

Some of these poems first appeared in the following publications: *Fort Necessity*, *Greetings*, *The Hat*, *Hanging Loose*, *LIT*, *New American Writing*, and *Sonora Review*. Special thanks to Askold Melnyczuk, Fiona McCrae, and Jeff Shotts for featuring some of these poems in *Take Three 3: AGNI New Poets Series* (AGNI/Graywolf Press, 1998), and to Todd Colby for including several in *Heights of the Marvelous: A New York Anthology* (St. Martin's Press, 2000). Many thanks also to Cynthia Nelson, Lily Mazzarella, Jennie Portnof, Eileen Myles, David Lehman, Christina Crosby, Anne Greene, Robert Creeley, Annie Dillard, all the good people at the Graduate Center at CUNY, my family—Barbara, Dirk, Emily, and Kat—and last but not least, Mark Hitzges, for their incomparable assistance, intelligence, and inspiration.

Carnegie Hall

Shiner

I wake up growling apples and dirt
naked and stretched under a barn sky
I cannot recall how I hurt my right eye

Arch of vessels gone grape under the lid
An army of red ants, a cast of shadows.
Good God. My eye has gone weak. Simply

put, I walked into an opening door.
The world is constantly changing shape
very dangerous. Two desert tortoises

duke it out on Arizona soil. By morning
one's always left belly-up to boil.
Now you roll around with a rock

and see what kind of bruise you can muster
Dolefulness, caprice, regret, trauma
My bicycle has two seats get on

Carnegie Hall

Sometimes in life you need a little help Big Daddy
Free to compose something without tragedy
I note the screech of a limousine, your Irish eyes farewell!
Or *Wilkommen*! To timid rain, a ripple
on the flag of humiliation
All-beef dogs and luggage of innovation

Oh cross navigate puddles and disciplinary figures
I could mail myself as a violet
Recur as a nutritionist—
Monstrous
A beer's better than a woman because it don't get jealous
Shiny erect leg—a fake!
A jewel, a peach, hand in pocket. Thief!

Well it ain't the *doge* but we coalesce
around these golden doors, adroit figures
riding gargantuan fish
If I had a coin to toss as in the *Trevi*
but I am already returning
You're really pregnant, lady!
My hose casts a gray shadow

Turn of events, a veteran requests
no smoking at his table
in front of the ill-used cathedral
Roll tape—Golden Messiah, please let this move me
Rezando como no sabía—Yikes! Organs
terrify 6 pm at war with the rush hour moo

4

The organs win! Snap, snap, snap the Eucharist
with a dutiful Pentax as big steel pipes
sound off like slit mouths

Oh Trinity, Oh Cartier, Oh Hotel Dorset
Thick red flowers dying in a window display
Color so plush a peninsula
A gorgeous silver trumpet
steams up from the dermis
introducing the biscuit collection

I'm governed by a pair of functioning pumps
the white walk lights in dusk

Pendulous clovers of amber and onyx
I note that panhandling while eating potato chips
seems to reduce your chances

Voilà la Plaza and an array of vertical ties
Uh-oh Bomb-squad vans parked outside
I feel renegade and clairvoyant
amidst the secret securities
with doodads in their ears
Maybe it's the President again
outside the St. Moritz
I pause at the lovely liatus
The sweet autumn clematis

Deep gray night of gray felt folding
and enclosing explosions
Almost there, to Carnegie Hall
to see—who else?—Ravi Shankar

It's the Prime Minister of India
It's a perfect circle of electric light
It's an entwined raga round a daughter round a gata
It's my fiancé birthed out of dashing sudden night

Red-coated ushers swim
in a sea of silk saris
Usher me in, gentlemen
Raw silk the colors of arteries

September 2

Dragging around some miserable wife
on a real hike, straight up a cliff
of corn, holding onto silk husks
for dear life—it's a little odd
to vacation as your mistress, and as
the only one licensed to drive, but
no one seems to mind. A little
disturbed but making it through
Swelling up before noon, I dreamt
my abalone ring came apart
Live fish and shell peeled off
my finger, in a retail store
of which you were the owner.
This day smells like toast.

Wish Fulfillment

I saw Aurora bouncing down the street
in a thin gray undershirt, she had
no sense, she was a complete turnip,
her teeth flat and square like a horse's

I saw Aurora, a blood orange leaking
in the east, beast-like, internecine,
yet promising the best cinnamon rolls in town—
What a load of hog! Summer of love,

hie! Hie! Shake your grim baton, drag me
under your spell of ethereal porn—
Have you a turn of phrase? A bee
in your bonnet? Jargon? Sherry? Fine china?

Don't leave me with my hands full of snake!
he cries, then the sepia god stops by to confide
that he does not care if we think of him
as complex, simple, or not at all.

The good news is, in the history
of all this you will be remembered
as very handsome and deciduous.
Now let us target greed, regret,

fog-filled inlets, streets greased
with whiskey, any vulgar buds
in the garden of the unborn. Then
it all begins again with the bottom lock.

The World

The world is
reaching into
you deeper
and faster
and cheaper
than ever
before so
what do you
hope for an
afternoon
spent alone
with porn do
we live in a
world of
bodies or
not if the
falling trees
don't kill
the chimps
the lack of
habitat will
they squawk
as they swing
from branch
to branch
o-o-o-awak!
with those
miraculous

hands the
butterflies
killed off
by the new-
wave pollen
you can't hug
a Nazi and hope
he'll change
such an idea
is an affront
to national
security a child
stands O-mouthed
in a doorway
learning evil
a bomb makes
more shrapnel
if it explodes
on cement
so never let
your guard
down, not
for one
minute.

Everything is
muted and blue
the tip-tap of
creation seems
cloudy, not crisp

and words know
nothing more
than I do, or
they're not
telling. I grew
one seed, I
cultivated
one thing
a Christ-baby
who is what
he eats. A small
hot thing is
an animal that
smells good but
the good must
be sealed off
from the bad
or the bad
from the good
otherwise a
ghoulish black
vein might creep
up to the healthy
pink brain but
the earth is
molten and
made of
moods so
go ahead
blow it up

blow it up
your mouth
full of love
and anger
and white-
gold milk
a crack of
infinity will
pulse on in
one glistening
ovary so
believe
me, it's
the voice
of a miserable
motherfucker
that whispers
you cannot
realize
your
world

The Beginner

I didn't mean to hurt you, I am
a beginner beginning to lose

sight of what I was beginning, I am
beginning a house I am beginning

to grow filaments. I took you in, I took
you into my mouth into my hands I heard

the flutter of your creaseless heart
I heard your curls and your muscles

and the ongoing waft of detergent
Ka-boom, ka-boom

My heart, your heart
Two bodies, the color of egg

shifting under.

The Condemned Building

I lie all night
a lump of gum
sprouting knots
splayed as an encore
Your body missing, lifted
from the bed by bats
and carried up past
the fat yogurt moon
Mosquitoes smack
against the walls
and one stubby bulge
on the cactus refuses
to bloom. The city
will not release
its inhabitants, and dawn
is held back by a pin
At 5 am the fever breaks
runs around town
cries like a baby
A corona of hail renders
me speechless, as the crane
keeps dipping into the inferno
scooping out live cats and walls
I begin to pray, Come on
home honey, seek the Venus
under the sheet. Wake me
from the dream of the queen
who imprisons eunuchs

14

in soft white gowns
Make your bed of snow
in my mouth.

Times Square

Joy got lost, so lost
she couldn't find the sky.
If she doesn't live here,

who are all the lights for?
Who is doing the living?
Meanwhile the beige-suited chicks

have grown tired of it, all the Good War shit,
the drinks named after towns—
Fort Wayne, Rome, Pomfret.

This used to be
this whole block
something else entirely

The man in the hotel lobby gesticulates wildly
very near her breasts pushed upwards
in her blazer, their career

Amidst many hairless rubber animals for sale
and these hydrants, tropical juices, and
revolving kabobs, it's too hard to recall

which it was—that
all sadness is really anger
or all anger really sadness

now that everyone's out shopping
or out on parole, now that
the train doesn't stop here
anymore. Howdy, stranger.

Second Avenue, Winter

In the wintry mix guys are digging up
Second Avenue with monster-trucks. We

part ways after the flick—too violent
for our taste tonight, and now we're out

$8.75 all around. Bam! Bam! go the shots
in my head, but I'm too tired for danger

So I don't walk near the three guys
who have pulled over to piss on my block

I don't feel like seeing their pricks
at this late hour, nor walking through

their steaming streams of urine. At home
Stephen Hawking is aslant in his wheelchair

speaking through a box. He's telling us
about black holes. How they were discovered

on a blackboard. We may be waiting for
a signal sent one hundred years ago, and

it'll take one hundred more to get one back, so
how do we stay interested over that kind of time?

Now that there's no more wine, it's time for bed
What a comfort, to be less than a breath.

Sleepy Demise of the Season

Sleepy demise of the season
Pitching toward the greasy
heart of the next—what's

the difference—it's another
perfect day—violets trail
off in an innocent wind. We

walk around together because
we can. Let's be subsumed by
all of it, awaken to the cold

blue sun with a gurgle. While
our toes perch in this century,
and our torsos hurl into the next.

O glittering fiend! False spring!
Of course we're doomed to fail. But
we keep our passions, our luck proper.

On Turning 27

You have this many lines
to get it done—what?—
Delineate the undelineatable
i.e. cloud, motivation. This grid's
made of twigs. What makes it
"literature" is the illusion of
a burning house and the gradual
disappearance of sporty Italians
from the train. If I were in a bikini
and a "wrap" and slightly sandy
no surfers would really want to
"do me," how did it end so fast?
Thus I awake to my exfoliation
and the drama of the included.

A Misunderstanding

I thought Zen poems
were supposed to sound wise.

Now I'm going to buy
as much beer as five dollars

can buy and drink it
right here on the sofa.

Today's Snow

Today's snow is plaid, or the echo of plaid

Plaid coming down the stairs, dragging her ball and chain
shrugging off her mantle as if to say

Am I still pretty, or are you getting ready to discard me
into a heap of wet ash

Inside the air is stale, this building is what they call "a sick building"
which means for a century we'll be transmitting germs and our
    lackluster phrasing

Snow as a box of bubbles
Snow as barnacles on city umbrellas

Snow lining the caverns of sinuses
Snow on the Ditson Building

O snow of my snowless childhood
flickering like a wolf in and out of view

Make it new, everyone kept saying
so I gave up, and made it mine

Snow down in now, one blanket at a time
Snow like the prose of philosophy

Snow lands on two pendulous bronze acorns which are street lamps
curved away from each other like flowers with nothing more to say

Now diagonal again, a cat swapping its tail from side to side

What if we live in a snow-globe, a model of a cell, complete with
    floating mitochondria

What if all the flakes are ghosts each one with a message that
        floats down and melts unread
That would help to explain our dogged apprehension of tragedy

Straight down without mercy, plangent snow coats
the Italian caterers, Staples Express, a couple of metal benches

I am pretending not to know this snow is about to be slush, just
        one measly inch
no more than a guy in a green jumpsuit could push off the
        sidewalk with a hoe, which he does

The Topers

In *El Triunfo de Baco* he looks sad
for us—for we who are too stupid

to be sad for ourselves. It's in his
ivory pudge, it's in his ivy crown.

Who else is sad for us—
Grandpa Baker down in Mississippi

who truly believes Jesus was sipping
grape punch at his last trough. What's

shocking, beyond this puffiness,
is that night is actually

quite generous. It knows something
we don't, as did Bacchus. It's only

Velazquez who sat around fussing
with the charcoal gray sky, it's

Velazquez who lived and died.

Eighteen Days Until Christmas

I lost the romance of this place
and woke up old. One darling
fantasy shattered over the next,
folding over a fist drenched
in my hip. The Christmas trees
are bound and stacked up
outside, the air can't decide
what to make of itself, and we
are about to throw a president
out. You are not your mother,
and each of your dead lives on
in you and smells like the moon.
Large and mosquito-like,
my prose clatters off
my fingers. I woke up old
and into happy uncertainty,
the vitamins I feed to the streets,
the real relations within a bead.
Oh pouring cylinder, stark
uncertainty, racket of leaves
helicoptering to their death—
my love is coming out
over and over again.
Here it is, what
I always wanted. The air
spills ash; I suppose
it is light.

Harbor

Light Slab Big on the Pillow

Time to get up and stare
at wasted space, slow-roasted greenery
Slim beige bird, my master

It's high school again and too many people
are piling into one car, we're forced
to express ourselves in modern dance

The loft where we used to fuck
is inhabited by a dead elf; the dials
in the auto have all stopped

Actually the elf is alive, just melodramatic
and the carnival has to take to the sea.
Mon enfant takes notes, from a distance.

Molino

I wandered through the pills of light
Fat light on the wainscoting, then

shadows on the landing, shadows
an itch in an otherwise compound eye

In summer when fog is furniture
a blade pushed through the bush

to reveal a diving hole, I rigged
a rope and swung out, smashed

the surface of what we don't own
and call home. Tall home, cold home,

home made of vines. X marks
the spot where X died. A rope swung

out, a rope swung high, then sex
with a hitchhiker I named Sky. Things

too small for the smallest boxes
Eerie sonatas, totems of marijuana,

body-crumbs bodies leave behind.
Fool's gold fills the pan, only a fool

would ask why. After seventeen seconds,
each second equal to one day, the shaking

ceased. The blue forest stood up,
walked away.

Wheels

You can't have anything forever
not your bride nor your skin
not even your trusty Volkswagen.

The joke is on us—the body
in the bed may not be a body at all
but bed made to look like body.

When you thought a beloved
was about to enter, it wouldn't
have mattered. They were all actors.

Sometimes you need a prop
to go through with it. Other
times you need to stand among

low brown hills, empty-handed.
Oh perfect silver bug, you overheated
only once. I was seventeen

and driving back to the place
where I learned
how to be alone.

Zero

force it into
the inevitable
blind faith meets
idiot will

last dance of dumb
animals eating
their limbs off
though I was the only

one shrieking
as you walked away
into the night
of a thousand fates

into your one
gem fiction

January 27, 1984

Let me get the story straight.
He had gone to the ballet.

It had been beautiful.

He came home, sipped whiskey
and water, took off his glasses,

went to sleep.

He did not dream.
He did not get the morning paper.

He did not get the mail at three.

He did not get up to make dinner
and did not meet his evening date.

Earlier that day his ex-wife
had jogged to his house.

She had stood outside his bedroom window and wept.

She did not know he had died.
In fact she was crying because

they had divorced, and were still alive.

Later that night, as she tried
to rub heat back into his hands,

she understood what had come and gone.

There is no telling when a body
reaches its peak.

He did not dream, he did not shriek.

As far as I know the story,
he died in his sleep.

The Cord

What is the thing
we can love
together?

Maybe you, maybe
me, maybe
white wine.

You chart what perishes, find
its theme. I accumulate
daily, like a shelf.

If we could sit and say
nothing and both
love its music.

Vespers

Dusk comes down
like a dumbbell

shadowed with
orange. Don't be

so sensitive, it says,
you and your daddy cap

and untapped ore. In early evening
I remember how beautiful

you were, with your
aw-shucks face and

erotic blue eyes. Now
that I have nothing

in progress, I pass out
on scaffolds of cotton

and dream I have
as many hats as

hearts. O Bodhisattva,
when you appear to me

in your island get-up,
take me away from

my attachments
gently, don't leave

a burl that will grow
into a fat hunch. Trust

me, I'll hock it all
when the fire hits—

then when it's over,
we'll walk together

through the ashes, and star
our shoes with the bright

white metal.

For Lily on Her 25th Birthday

1.

You, the dark blue
of the sheet, the sin
she's guilty of, the ice-
crust of a Roman sea.
Sweet pea with a pacifier
of twigs and mulch, this
much you had—eyes of sea-
groped glass. Who you were
then I know now:
Eros kissing Psyche,
water over stones,
milk spilt over a rosary.

2.

Grown up and walking down the avenue
A walking stick of silk
Led by invisible chariots
or weeping in a cab
Sister why you so sad?
She who raged in you
made you ball up & turn blue
She was trying to cover up
the stench of wisdom.
It can't be done. You
are mother and dolphin in one,
a collage of lost evenings.

3.

Looking for you I wander
into awnings, hollering
at the sleet. It's you
who don't lie to me.
The slender gray cat
sniffing at the violets
stole your eyes, Lily,
as you slept. Left you
blind and soft as
the nugget at the root
of it all.

4.

Do you hear the captain
punching tickets? We're leaving
the station. We move in
and around large sounds.
Now, for the chalked-up meeting
of our hearts.

The Deep Blue Sea

for Robert Creeley

When I was smaller than I am today
I knew one kernel, one acorn-
hard thing.

There were hills, hills
more motherly than my mother
and wet sand that lived only

to get wetter. I was over-
whelmed, but knew the word
could balance on a finger.

When I read your poems
I drank the rain. I dug
my heels in, let weeping

root me. What wind there was
sped and hiccupped along
until I was dry, hung out on a line.

I mean what I say. You say
that's OK. So today I unknit
into wavy threads that play

at a grid, sometimes smutched
by a cruel and abstract plushness
Plush as what the rain ate

Plush as what small souls incarnate
You threw it out there, only hinted
where to look. I swam. Then up

it bobbed, one heart-
red buoy in the deep blue
sea. But winking at me.

The Ovals

for Dart

Waves of chunky snow
on the lake in winter,

the lighthouse a crease
in white air. Maybe the sand aches.

Blue eyes in a corridor of wrinkles,
drinks dirty with cherries. The death

of a woman soft as dough.
We reminisce.

Mind

The lilacs are starting to smell good
All things useless, gorgeous—
Terraces, composers, soup
It's good to see you. You tell me

about an old friend in California
huddled in a closet, his mind putty.
That mind, it was our friend. It took me
to the prom, it loved me.

Nothing howls in my skull these days
It's tranquil enough in there
Phosphenes of cornflower, lust
for running water, a throbbing lack

of historical fact. I don't even miss him,
and I see why you don't care. Where
we are when we can't help each other
is here. Lilacs swelling out of buckets,

people moving along. Half-empty,
half-full, or some fork
of the biological—Personally,
I don't ask for much more

than last Thursday, when
I wandered for hours
in the terrible rain
then arrived.

Vallejo

Fresh peaks of salt and pepper hair
amidst scratchy brine, barnacles
of sunshine and vermouth.
She looks about light! The ears
of a dead orchard, persimmons
knocked out by starlets.
My palm is soft confusion.
Sleep in the center of morning,
old jeans, strong coffee, a sister
to be found in gold whiskey and soap.
I am always a child here, my mother
smooth and small. I crawl along
the isthmus, the wet pasture
of egrets, the softness
that would be water.
It is a fever of bread, that would be
coarseness. It is an orange heart
that rests in my palm.
The hills are nothing
if not reception.

After the Holidays

for Tara Jane O'Neil

Everything conspires to make this journey go fast
the jet stream, the in-flight entertainment, etc.

When really the sky and sea frenching into the sorry sand
is all I want to think about, and the slippery red sun going down

A sea lion bobbing in the waves
Hold on a minute, onto these long smoke wings

Holidays with family remind me of the saying
Guilt is the gift that keeps on giving

Yes I am guilty, if a fly dies in Mongolia,
if you suddenly find yourself without Kleenex

Beautiful winter, I'm happy to see you
after twelve perfect-days-for-a-hike

and you too, lp of aching beauty
O beauty, what do you do with it

after crying wolf about it for so long?
Let it turn into an overgrown lot

Put a firecracker up its arse
What do you say, Mr. Kind Eyes?

Your swollen sinus headache prohibits sex
and that's too bad as I have a fever

swelling up my cheeks breaking
vessels in the fragile corners

the same Swedish cheeks I see on sweet Emily
who is my sister and also a hybrid camellia

O thumb piano
so cute and naive

Thank you for making music
for my homecoming

Harbor

Not quite at home in the world
and turning toward the terminus

Night-swimming with my sister
who stays back by the shore

The force that gets the body
out of the soul

What's personal is what you hold
in your hand

A bottle of catsup
The pour of green water

If I were to escape beauty
into the season of giving

I would give to the birds,
the sad, and the leaning.

I would use simple language
to describe the forest. Failing that,

I'd find a piano.
Nickel body, nickel world

You are a figure illuminated
from behind by a light.

The underbelly of sunset
The rattling of blue logs.

The house is over. That is,
what you never went back for

has been loaded into a dumpster.
A bridge is an arc of green lights

over black water. This is memory
weather, and I remember

the roof in summer. How it stood.
How we stood upon it.

After All

Sunday Night

Choose. If you want
meditation or poppy

or something altogether uncouth—
my riffle to your raffle

red façade to red façade
angel bucking sordid angel

Or why not make a malt of it? It's
virtually the same thing as a milkshake

but with powder. Powder is what's left
after the ideas have died. The sago palm

uncurls a new green hand into night. A truck
the size of Wisconsin drops off an acre

of rich mushroom compost in the yard
Let's get deep into it, make it our beard

Never fear, never fear, not while
the crescent moon is here, a crooked

smile of luminous jest. No matter what
happens next, remember this:

If a rice gets lonely, it will die.

A History

I turned away then, away
from our soft contours
the miracle the sea makes
with shards of glass

You as you were when I abandoned you
a spray of blue, a moistness
supple albino flesh carved and marked
by a variety of fingers

Now the pressure's really on
to notice something new:
the brush dipping in brown
about to slice a horizon;

the flap between shade and sill,
carnivorous. The tinkling
builds to a roar. You
were adored, do you hear,

adored. Quietly I admit
something to myself, something
I hope to remember.

Roses

Impossibly soft and pink
Damn it they open! Open
and fall to pieces. As
I might do on a more wanton
afternoon. Lush, indifferent,
about to go bad. Meanwhile
we walk around feeling fat
and I've got a summer rash.
I want to be as uniformly pink
to you, but what with
these noontime shit-tones of
avocado, coffee, the smash-up
of peace. The rain pitters
and moves on, denying the city
the deluge it needs. I fear
you letting me fly back
to the fretless life
I no longer want or could be.
Proof, proof you loved me
enough in one moment
to sweeten a whole life:
twelve stems and one
decent knife. Oh roses,
enough said. To learn
from their death how
to live beside you,
equally halting
and opened.

After Rilke (II, 28)

Oh common gaze. Ersatz
August of taut fingers.
Even the queen of feathers
was born from ordinary nature.

When the gang has you licked,
do not surrender. In your
worst night of dying damsels,
weep, but also befriend a tree.

Do not let them gore you of Zen
in that worst night, gondolier!
Hobble through the grit

thy vest made of spritzer,
hops, and the sun's tears.
There, in the back country of friends.

Nirvana

Dank blossoms making their way
into nothingness
The pink path where we lie
bear-hugging the good-smelling dirt

Kids roll down the grassy hills
like Tootsie Rolls but shrieking
The sun tucks us all in
to oblivion

Orbs fly at us, purple feathers
shock us by fluttering
off the screen
and landing nearby

Are they laser feathers, or
feathers made by my eye
or intruders blown out of soft water
crying *cocaine, cocaine*

The children sleep like capsules
hot capsules in the sun
Pick one up, a bag of darling
Just get your body down to the good-smelling dirt

Here's where things with shells live
Here's where we nap wholesomely
Here's where the dreams come home,
come home to roost.

Nap

Alarm
beats from day to
night, your hands folded up
like griffins. Wind howls outside,
jostles

the stores.
Long shirt, naked
below the waist, you dream
into the winter night. That's right,
dream so

you won't
have to be the
alarmist at heart, the
girl with darts. The pet rock. The plung-
ing wall.

Another Waitressing Dream

I'll have the jack pie
he said, and I went
to write it down
on my pad

Then I said, we don't
have jack pie, we have
apple, pecan, cherry,
or key lime

Well I want jack pie,
he said, and I began
to suspect I was
being had

After Talking Late with Friends and a Line by T'ao Ch'ien

On this day of shattering rain,
the planes fly low. Who am I

to ask such questions
of those I know? Their answers

confound me, as does the muscle
of the elbow, the one that pushes the pose

skyward. Hoping to be treasured
and later, remembered

is the kind of folly
this rain moves out. Mad rain,

that finds these recurring ideas
a new home.

After a Fight

Fuck you too, my less compassionate self
says quietly. You've never really

respected me anyway, especially not now
that I refuse to be the keeper

of your anger, the messy pall
of it, from where we kill

what we can't suck. Still
I have faith in the healthy ink

of ideograms, the little cone of flame
nudged about by the wind.

My pillow book would list
such beautiful things, your heart

would die to read them.

The Pool

One world, many people in it.
Strong Paul, the professional woman

in the white cap, the Korean man
with the beautiful butterfly, the hipster

with an eye tattooed on top of each
of his feet. I watch their forms lewdly

as they waver in the orange and blue light
& whisper underwater   *I love you when you swim*

Winding Down

Everyone's life seems to have more meaning than mine
now that I'm just through scooting around

with platters of food, nothing really on my mind
I've got to go all the way to motherfucking Brooklyn

my cabby complains to his cell phone, while back at home
the wind is wild, it pins plastic bags against an old dead fridge

lying on its side, it's garbage night. I find that an ex
has posted photos of his newborn on the web

It's the new thing to do, the baby has his eyes
I wouldn't do it, what I would do

is be a wafer if it weren't for the sun which is about to come up
You say you're hungry for my body but what does that mean

Is it the way I want to be one
of the orange chunky clouds getting

whipped around? The wind whips everything
around tonight, it has a will, it is crisp and regal

Only the constellations stay put, flat white
pinups, always playing it cool.

Apology

It isn't the unplayed game
of call-and-response
or even my pissy
anger, as much as

the fact that our limitations
couldn't be fixed
with a hammer. Now
if my love could do

anything right, it
would be as soft
to you as today's
snow and candles.

Proposal

1.

Awoken: two eyes home
to an immigrant sadness,
right reason swallowed
by dolphins. Grown-up
back to you, belly to you,
womanly. Whose skin
is this? Whose desire?
Newly-arranged organs
inarticulate and dazzling
This is why I stagger
This is how I sing.

2.

Dizzy with the sound of hands
every morning, every night.
Dirty silt swirls into an eddy
then re-routes itself
to the merciless sea.
Consecrate me. I know
you hear the darkness
in me, and the tread
of light on lake.

3.

Turning to the indelible present
No gout, no weeds.
Designed by a want
free of gluttony
yet clenching and stretching
like ivy. What gesture
could I make to be
most wise-mannered,
most true? To stand,
stand guard over
your solitude.

4.

Swelling calligraphy, the meat
of our lives
Absolute draw of ever
Dreams and demons
broken with sugars
file one by one
out of the chamber
walk rawly into day
a day unattuned to these tremors,
our one-armed climb
to the cave. I had
to hurl myself
onto the boat, a newborn
desperate for protein,
a loose leaf.

5.

Aching for fanatics
and the ailing planet
Soldiers of God or
butchers with eyes
of cloud. The sight
of a poverty that might
change your life. Smack,
smack, you crack
eggs against chrome.
I return to our conversation
saddened, of things
of myself, of things
made of stone.

6.

I propose the obliteration
of nomination, I propose
sea. I propose
the axing of schemata,
the arrival of a hail
no one else can see.
I propose strings.
Your quiet eyes.

7.

The literal foils us
when we grasp at it most:
incredulity, agitation,
remnants of some past
degradation. In this
shallow hot space
of summer, forget
the eye of the beholder.
We are awash in a fog
of deities, a hill
of laughing melon.

8.

Mare-eyed fiend trickling
to me, weep the weight
of your stroke that must be
endured. Smashing
the aimless gray
the violence you might
have housed, egged on
by absorbent paper.
The boundless becoming bound
the color of the meek.
Unable to protect you
from such things,
I offer incarnation.

9.

Age of impatiences. Denies
ripening. Still all that lives
fights for life. I babble
all night of promises,
of sacrifice. The stain
of incoherence somehow
seems a home, with its
cellos, its swing-lows,
its fig-edged sheets.

10.

Close air circling the bicep
of another O-mouthed morning
These moods are paper tigers
swaying in an absent breeze.
Skin off the shoulder
of a constellation
we cannot foresee, skin
of the selves we've been.
I enter the crescendo
of those images, feel
the chariot that has driven
your hands. Light another,
another crinkling thing
doomed to burn up, then
be pondered. No.
I want to love you nobly,
then be forgotten.

This is how it goes, then,
the walk toward
union.

Still Life

for Mark

Dull glass
can barely
make out
night, red
hands of
a clock
separate
us, now
a lush
peony
climaxes in
silence.
Penny for
your thoughts,
sister. There
are the
apples we
bought on
Saturday.

I twinkle
across the
distance, not
really knowing
your point of
view. Are we
the glass

the world pours
into, or is it
our love that
saturates
the world? Do
tell, my friend,
by day when
the phone
starts ringing
and you are
mine in no
time.

Losing Heart

It feels good
like being
inside a car
in a car

wash, the froth
swopping
the roof, the
windows, a regular

murder of dirt.
But what if
it's the self
at stake, not

crimson with sin
just weary of
its own
contours, the run-on

sentence of its
thought. On
the inside looking
out, a window

streaked with black
effluvia, always
threatening to
become a hunk of

something that
won't budge. When
I was a younger man
it was all about

Mozart. Then later,
Beethoven. Then
later still—Mozart!
After that, Beethoven!

Ah, but Mozart. Ah,
but Beethoven.
You don't really

have to believe in
yourself, only
in your circulation.

After All

So night may not be an adventure—
the *brio* you'd have given

your life for
(the pantry, the tea, the indoor cat)

drops down, a bean
through a funnel.

I'm talking to you!
But the alley is stillborn,

lit by a dusk
that won't hold hands,

only promises to move along
and be blue.

Subway in March, 5:45 pm

I take the long way home, knowing
I am free to choose happiness

or wander off into the tunnel
On the platform two teenagers french kiss, her lips

are enormous and soft and he seems at home with them
I feel crumpled like the pastel houses lining the canal

I am transporting an adorable succulent
the size of an infant's fist, holding it close as if

it were the one thing I had to keep alive
and thinking how much easier it would be

if all I had to love were this small plant
and then I wouldn't be so hard on you

and we could like the world before distrusting it
Stop performing ourselves and let the pith of us

hang out. All these permutations of esteem and ridicule
when all I want is to stay focused on everyday life

What other kind of life is there?
All the world knows it, it's a miracle

The blue womb of evening
The nimble sparrow, the smug duck in the pond

The eruption of flowering quince
O shackle us to the rock of it

we will try to love each other
though there's wind on our heads

and we cannot read minds
The train jumps above ground

and stripes the car in gold light
It's the light of early spring

ZED

Zed is a platform for marginalised voices across the globe.

It is the world's largest publishing collective and a world leading example of alternative, non-hierarchical business practice.

It has no CEO, no MD and no bosses and is owned and managed by its workers who are all on equal pay.

It makes its content available in as many languages as possible.

It publishes content critical of oppressive power structures and regimes.

It publishes content that changes its readers' thinking.

It publishes content that other publishers won't and that the establishment finds threatening.

It has been subject to repeated acts of censorship by states and corporations.

It fights all forms of censorship.

It is financially and ideologically independent of any party, corporation, state or individual.

Its books are shared all over the world.

www.zedbooks.net
@ZedBooks